SPECIAL FORCES

Jim Brush

FRANKLIN WATTS

LONDON·SYDNEY

First published in 2010 by
Franklin Watts
338 Euston Road
London NW1 3BH

Franklin Watts Australia
Level 17/207 Kent Street
Sydney NSW 2000

Series editor: Adrian Cole
Art director: Jonathan Hair
Design: Simon Borrough
Picture research: Luped

Acknowledgements:
AP / Press Association Images: 28t; Boeing: 23bl, 40c; Capt. Tommy Avilucea / Press Association: 7t; Chris Hondros / Getty Images: 34t; Chung Sung-Jun / Getty Images: 33c; Corbis: 6cr; Courtesy of American Technologies Network Corporation: 23br; Courtesy of Commonwealth of Australia: 9t, 12b; Courtesy of Thales Group: 33t; Cpl. Andrew S. Avitt / Photo Courtesy of U.S. Army: 11c; David Rubinger / Corbis: 29b; Don Montgomery / Photo Courtesy of U.S. Navy: 41t; Echoart / Dreamstime.com: 22cr; Getty Images: 29t; Greg E. Mathieson / Rex Features: 6tc, 10b, 15c, 22cl; ImageWorks / TopFoto: 34c; Jeffrey Allen / USAF / Getty Images: 31t; Jim Gallagher / Crown Copyright / MOD: 41b; John Moore / Getty Images: 25b; Jordi Chias / TopFoto: 37t; Leif Skoogfors / Corbis: 12c, 18t; Mass Communication Specialist 1st Class Roger S. Duncan / Photo Courtesy of U.S. Navy: 20b, 44b; Mass Communication Specialist 2nd Class Dominique M. Lasco / Photo Courtesy of U.S. Navy: 17tl; Mass Communication Specialist 2nd Class Erika N. Jones / Photo Courtesy of U.S. Navy: 14l; MC2 Michelle Kapica / Photo Courtesy of U.S. Navy: 15t; Nina Shannon / iStockphoto: 22tr; Omeo Gacad / AFP / Getty Images: 35t; Patrick Chauvel / Sygma / Corbis: 32t; Paul Melcher / Rex Features: 23t; Paula Bronstein / Getty Images: 19b; Pedro Jorge Henriques Monteiro / Shutterstock: Front Cover; Photo Courtesy of U.S. Army: 10tr; Photo Courtesy of U.S. Army / Tech. Sgt. Jerry Morrison: 8c; Photo Courtesy of U.S. Navy: 6cl; Photographer's Mate 2nd Class Eric S. Logsdon / Photo Courtesy of U.S. Navy: 3, 15bl, 36b; Photographer's Mate 1st Class Arlo Abrahamson / Photo Courtesy of U.S. Navy: 17br, 44t; Reuters / Corbis: 16c; Robert Nickelsberg / Getty Images: 9bl; Scott Nelson / Getty Images: 13c; SFC Andrew Kosterman / Photo Courtesy of U.S. Army: 26b; Sgt. David N. Gunn / Photo Courtesy of U.S. Army: 35c; Sipa Press / Rex Features: 27b, 39c; Spc. Michael J. MacLeod / Photo Courtesy of U.S. Army: 24b; Staff Sgt. Jeremy T. Lock / Photo Courtesy of U.S. Navy: 30b, 45; Stephanie McGehee / Reuters: 21b; Sukree Sukplang / Reuters / Corbis: 21tl; USASOC / Photo Courtesy of U.S. Army: 25t, 38b; Wessel Du Plooy / iStockphoto: 26c; Won Dai-Yeon / AFP / Getty Images: 36c.

A CIP catalogue record for this book is available from the British Library.

Dewey number: 355'.03

ISBN: 978 0 7496 9352 7

Printed in China

Franklin Watts is a division of Hachette Children's Books, an Hachette UK company.
www.hachette.co.uk

Author's note:
Some soldiers' faces in this book have been blurred to protect the identities of people still serving in the Special Forces.

Contents

Words highlighted in the text can be found in the glossary.

Swords of lightning

This is the 'sword of lightning' badge of US Army Green Berets.

Special Forces are small groups of highly-trained soldiers. They operate unseen and unheard behind enemy lines. Their enemies never know when or where they will strike.

This is the badge of US Navy SEALs. It shows an eagle holding a pistol, anchor and trident.

AF FACTS

Among the most famous Special Forces in the world are the British SAS (Special Air Service), the US Delta Force, SEALs, Green Berets and Rangers, and the French Foreign Legion and Force d'Action Rapide (FAR).

US Army Rangers using computers and communications equipment behind enemy lines.

Today, there are few large wars in the world, but there are many smaller **conflicts**. Special Forces teams strike hard and fast, like 'swords of lightning'. They can carry out an important mission without a country needing to send a large armed force.

US-trained Iraqi Special Forces carry out a hostage rescue training mission in Baghdad.

Special Forces teams are also used to deal with threats from terrorists, pirates or well-armed criminal gangs. US Special Forces also train local security forces to prevent attacks. Iraqi Special Forces have been trained to help prevent government officials being killed or kidnapped.

ACTION STATS

The United States has the largest Special Forces – around 55,000 members in 2009. This number includes cooks, medics, mechanics, supply teams and many other roles as well as fighting soldiers.

"I accept the fact that as a Ranger my country expects me to move farther, faster and fight harder than any other soldier."
US Army Ranger Code

Who are they?

Special Forces troops include men recruited from civilian life and from other armed services. They have years of training and experience. All candidates have to be physically and mentally tough, intelligent, skilful and resourceful. They are the best at what they do.

A Special Forces team practise attacking an enemy base.

AF FACTS

The British SAS is divided into units, each with their own special skills. There is a Boat Troop (diving), an Air Troop (parachute), Mountain Troop (skiing) and Mobility Troop (long range patrols).

Special Forces patrols are expected to fight against much larger forces. They must train harder than almost any other soldiers. Their motto is "train hard, fight easy". But they do a lot more than just fight. They need radio and language skills, first-aid training, plus **tactical** and survival skills to stay alive in tough environments.

This is the new MH-53J, equipped with an **infra-red** system for night flights.

Special Forces teams usually work in secret. They are rarely seen by reporters or TV crews. Often the only way we know about their missions is after they have happened, or if any of the unit is killed during the mission.

Some Special Forces units are rarely seen. This **sniper** is wearing a ghillie suit which has twigs and leaves added to help hide him

"These guys are putting their lives on the line, taking on some very serious bad guys. The less anyone knows about the unit, the better."
Delta Force soldier

What do they do?

Special Forces teams are sent on the most difficult missions. Some operate surrounded by the enemy without being seen for long periods. Others strike from the air or sea and leave again quickly.

A squad in desert gear prepare for direct action (see left).

In battle, Special Forces teams have two main jobs. The first is scouting, or **reconnaissance**. They operate behind enemy lines and gather information from the enemy. Their second job is to attack enemy strong points, called direct action, before the main battle.

Members of the US 10th Mountain Division operate in tough conditions. These troops are wearing snow gear.

AF FACTS

Some Special Forces troops fight wearing uniforms. They use special tactics and camouflage to stay hidden. Other troops blend in with local people by wearing clothes like theirs.

Special Forces teams often have to fight while keeping other people safe. For example, during a hostage rescue mission it can be hard to shoot at kidnappers without harming the hostages. It can be a race against time to get them out alive.

These troops from Thailand are being trained to use explosives by a US Special Forces team.

AF FACTS

US Special Forces help to train other security forces. In Iraq, many US soldiers learned to speak the local language to help them communicate.

"Anyone can just go in there and kill someone, but you can't get information from a corpse."
US Navy SEALs motto

Where do they fight?

Special Forces troops must be prepared to go anywhere in the world. Units are often sent on a mission at short notice in all sorts of terrain.

US Navy SEALs on patrol in Panama. They are part of a Special Boat Unit (see pages 36–37).

Australian Special Forces soldiers on patrol in Afghanistan.

Some Special Forces troops attack from the sea in fast boats, while others go into action by jumping out of planes. They operate in some of the wildest terrains on Earth: steamy jungles, scorching deserts or icy mountains.

US Special Forces soldiers use horses in Afghanistan to patrol areas where trucks cannot reach.

At all times, Special Forces troops must adapt to what is around them. In 2002, members of the US Special Forces in Afghanistan rode around on horses. There were few roads, so it was the quickest way to move through the mountains.

ACTION STATS

One problem for Special Forces teams is carrying enough food to eat. Fighting in the jungles of Borneo during the 1960s, Australian SAS troops lost up to 4 kg in weight after a 12-day patrol.

Tough training

Basic training is very intense and can last many months. The first stage is fitness. Tough exercises include running, swimming and long marches at night.

During training, **recruits** are given very few clues about what's in store for them the next day. A blackboard in the camp gives instructions, such as: "Red 3 report to vehicle at 0700 hours with full kit and a 22 kg pack." Recruits are tested on their own and in teams to see how well they cope.

ACTION-STATS

Recruits wishing to join the US Delta Force must go on a 65 km march in two days, with little or no sleep. SAS candidates have to climb an 880-metre high peak three times in four hours.

This recruit is just finishing an 8-km hike as part of a 15-week training programme, before moving on to the next stage.

"On the first couple of speed marches, I only reached the end by being carried by the front men. I was exhausted." British Parachute Regiment soldier

Recruits power their way through the surf on another training exercise.

Recruits attempt to swim 100 metres (m) with their hands tied. (Don't try this yourself!)

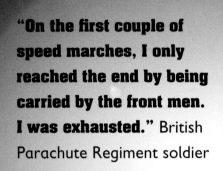

Training is not just about fitness. During SEALs 'Hell Week' (above) recruits are taught the importance of listening to instructions.

AF FACTS

Only the best soldiers get to join Special Forces teams. Around 80% of candidates who apply or go through training are rejected.

Skills training

The second stage of training is six months of basic skills. Recruits learn how to move behind enemy lines, how to use different weapons and how to work in teams.

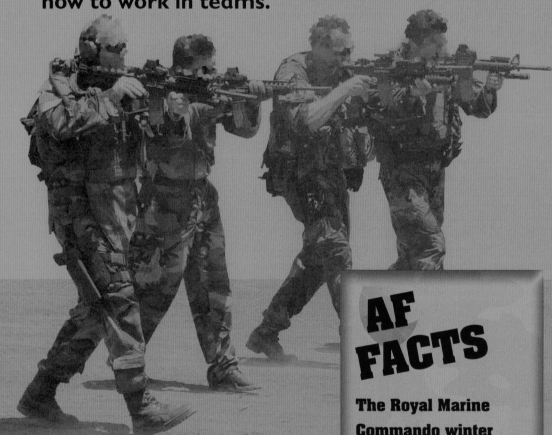

Members of the US Army Special Forces show how to target the enemy while moving.

Special Forces recruits can spend over 1,000 hours of training just on the shooting range. They are also trained in basic first aid, tactics, using a radio and handling enemy weapons.

AF FACTS

The Royal Marine Commando winter warfare course includes a 300 km-long patrol. Recruits must ski through 'enemy' territory, collecting information for later raids.

AF FACTS

Recruits in the South African Special Forces, the 'Recces', are taught bushcraft. They learn how to build shelters and deal with wild animals, bush fires and stinging insects (see page 20).

Not only are recruits taught how to use radios to communicate, but also how to plot positions on maps and how to find their way there.

The third and final stage of training is learning specialist skills, such as sniping, explosives, jungle warfare or using a parachute. Some troops focus on learning how to drive in woods, deserts or in the mountains.

Skills training includes learning to use special vehicles, such as this Desert Patrol Vehicle (DPV).

"We aren't going to try to train you, we're going to try to kill you." SAS training instructor

Unseen and unheard

This sniper is so well camouflaged it is only possible to see his rifle.

One of the most important Special Forces' skills is learning how to stay hidden. Their uniforms have colours and patterns – called camouflage – that blend in with what's around them.

Special Forces troops learn the art of camouflage to help them hide. Floppy hats and branches threaded into their equipment change their shape. Shiny metal surfaces are taped up. Dark camouflage cream is smeared onto faces and hands.

"**Most members of the Special Forces could walk into a shop and nobody would notice anything unusual about them.**"
Special Forces' officer

Recruits also learn how to avoid capture and how to escape from the enemy if caught. SAS recruits take part in a 5-day escape exercise in the Brecon Beacons in Wales.

AF FACTS

In the jungle, patrols give themselves the 'jump' test. They jump up and down to see if any equipment rattles. A squeaky boot or noisy water bottle could easily alert the enemy.

Some Special Forces soldiers wear regular uniforms. These ones are driving around in a pick-up truck.

AF FACTS

When the SAS was first formed in the 1950s, recruits improved their stalking skills using air rifles and wearing fencing masks. Today, recruits in the USA train using laser and computer-operated battle systems.

Survival skills

Special Forces soldiers must be able to survive behind enemy lines with little or no support. They are trained to find and build shelters and to locate food and water.

Shelters can range from a snow cave to a ditch covered in branches. Soldiers are also trained to light fires without matches. They must be able to find clean drinking water, and to live on fruit, nuts, roots and wild animals. The US Green Berets' nickname, 'Snake-eaters', comes from their survival course.

Making a warm fire in a frozen environment is just one of the key survival skills.

ACTION STATS

During the 1950s, one SAS patrol in Malaya (now Malaysia) spent 103 days in a row in the jungle.

"My patrol commander was bitten on the arm by a scorpion and within a few hours you would swear that someone had slipped a football under his skin. It was huge!"

Ian Conaghan, SAS trooper in the jungles of Borneo

A soldier catches a snake as part of a survival challenge.

Keeping weapons ready to use is another important survival skill.

Basic kit

Most Special Forces units carry the basic equipment, such as a rifle, body armour and a compass. They also carry electronic gadgets to help them fight at night or find their position.

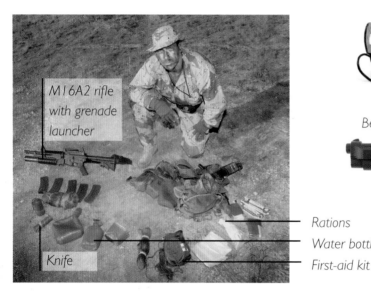

M16A2 rifle with grenade launcher

Knife

Rations

Water bottle

First-aid kit

Compass

Beretta 9 mm pistol

Every team member carries a weapon for the specific mission, such as an M4 assault rifle, M24 sniper rifle or Beretta 9 mm pistol. They also carry a combat knife which can be used for hand-to-hand fighting (see right). As well as bringing water and rations (food), they also carry spare **ammunition** and radio batteries.

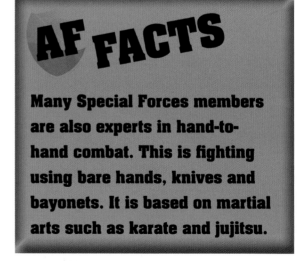

AF FACTS

Many Special Forces members are also experts in hand-to-hand combat. This is fighting using bare hands, knives and bayonets. It is based on martial arts such as karate and jujitsu.

ACTION STATS

Satellite smart phones, like this one, provide connections to military GPS networks.

A Global Positioning System, or GPS, shows a team's location, time and speed. It uses signals from satellites in space. Wherever you are on Earth, it can show where you are standing within 50 m!

Each team also has a GPS (see left). Radios and satellite phones are used to keep in touch with base. Night-vision goggles are used by teams to see when they operate in the dark. Other equipment, such as the CSEL (see below left) can help units when they are in trouble.

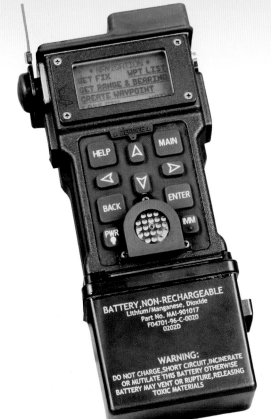

Night-vision goggles

The Combat Survivor Evader Locator (CSEL) uses a satellite network to link units on the ground with support and rescue teams back at base.

Heavy weapons

As well as their basic kit, a typical eight-man Special Forces patrol carries more weapons than a hundred soldiers in the regular army.

ACTION STATS

The M320 grenade launcher fires single shot 40 mm shells: explosive or smoke. The version below is fitted with a laser rangefinder and a day or night sight – so it can also be used in the dark.

Bigger weapons include grenade launchers, a heavy machine gun and an anti-tank weapon. Members of the unit take it in turns to carry this heavy equipment along with mines, a first-aid kit and a set of explosives.

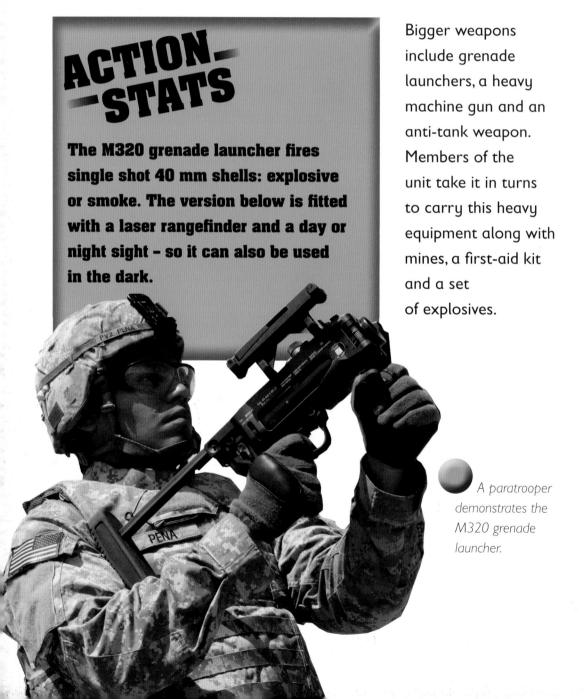

A paratrooper demonstrates the M320 grenade launcher.

Mines, such as the one shown here, are powerful explosive weapons.

If all this isn't enough, Special Forces patrols are often supported by aircraft or helicopters, warships or army **artillery**. The patrols use their radio, for example, to give the location of an enemy base or a bridge that needs to be destroyed.

One of the most powerful weapons available to a Special Forces team is their radio. They can call in **airstrikes**, like the one below, and artillery support.

Helicopter drops

A common way for Special Forces patrols to get behind enemy lines is to be dropped and picked up by small groups of helicopters.

A helicopter's ability to land and take-off in a small space helps Special Forces patrols land in secret locations. Helicopters can fly in all weathers, both night and day. They can also rescue patrols quickly if they get into trouble.

Five Puma helicopters take-off on a mission, followed by their armed support – Apache attack helicopters.

ACTION-STATS

A CH-47 Chinook heavy-lifting helicopter can carry over 50 Special Forces troops in one flight. The MH-47D is used by US Special Forces and can be refuelled in flight.

US 1st Special Forces soldiers drop into the sea from a hovering MH-47D Chinook.

During Operation Telic in 2003, 97 Puma and Lynx helicopters landed 1,500 Royal Marine Commandos close to the Iraqi coastline. It took great skill to fly close to the ground at night through sand and dust storms.

"Night dust landings were very difficult, despite having experienced soldiers." Major General David H. Petreaus, commander of US 101st Airborne Division

ACTION STATS

A Puma helicopter can operate day and night (when the crew wear night-vision goggles). It can carry 16 fully-equipped troops or two tonnes of cargo. Six stretchers can be fitted for picking up wounded soldiers.

French commandos are dropped off by a Puma helicopter.

Mission: Operation Thunderbolt

Many Special Forces teams are experts at rescuing hostages that have been kidnapped by terrorists.

One of the most famous hostage rescues took place in 1976. Terrorists seized 258 passengers of Air France flight 139 (similar to the plane above) from Tel Aviv in Israel to Paris. Israeli Special Forces teams followed the plane over 5,000 km to Entebbe airport in the African country of Uganda.

AF FACTS

The Israeli Special Forces team built a replica of part of the airport building. They practised their attack on the terminal where the hostages were being held.

Israeli Special Forces during a training exercise in the 1970s.

On Saturday 3 July, Operation Thunderbolt went ahead. The whole attack lasted just 53 minutes. In that time, eight hijackers were killed. Of the remaining 105 hostages, one was killed by the terrorists and two more by accident. The rest were rescued and flown back to Israel.

ACTION STATS

To avoid being detected by radar, the four Hercules C-130 planes carrying the Israeli Special Forces flew at a height of less than 30 m over the Red Sea.

A crowd celebrates the return of the hostages in Israel — lifting one of the pilots into the air.

Jumping into action

One of the main ways for Special Forces patrols to arrive in secret is to jump from planes at night. Using parachutes, they can glide quietly to the ground.

A squad carry out a HALO jump at 3,600 m.

In High Altitude, Low Opening (HALO) jumps, teams jump out of the plane up to 10,000 m in the air. They make their body into a wing shape and 'fly' towards their meeting point at speeds of over 240 kph. At a set height, their parachute opens to slow their fall.

Members of the British Forces Special Tactics squad parachute to the ground following a HALO jump.

In High Altitude, High Opening (HAHO) jumps, the parachutes open straight away. This allows the team to glide up to 50 km from their drop position. Special strips on top of the parachute allow members of the team to see each other.

AF FACTS

Troops that parachute into the jungle wear a special harness. This allows them to parachute into the treetops, then lower themselves to the ground.

"The landing sites were usually chosen from a map... Whether you could land or not, you would never know until you got there."
NZ Special Forces trooper

Mountain and mobility

A soldier from Force d'Action Rapide lies ready for action in a snow-covered hole.

Mountain units – or mobility troops – specialise in mountain and arctic warfare. They are expert climbers and skiers. They can also handle a variety of vehicles, from a sledge to a snowmobile.

Mountain units are trained to make parachute jumps into the snow. They also learn skills such as cutting trails through snow, rock climbing and sliding down ropes, called abseiling. They also learn to 'mountain walk', where they step over obstacles that could fall or cause **avalanches**.

South Korean Special Warfare Forces ski during a snowy mountain exercise.

ACTION STATS

Mobility troops are experts in using vehicles for hit-and-run attacks. They also have excellent desert survival skills. Each member needs to drink 9 litres of water per day because of the hot sun. They often travel at night to stay hidden, and because it is cooler.

Mission: Cave fighting

In 2001, US and British Special Forces teams were sent to attack terrorist training camps inside Afghanistan.

Part of a destroyed cave suspected of being part of an underground training camp.

Members of US 3rd Special Forces Group watch out for enemy forces in Afghanistan.

It was a difficult mission but the teams had to work fast, as winter was on its way. Many of the terrorist camps were inside large caves that were hard to spot from the air. Special Forces patrols on the ground found the caves, then called in planes for an airstrike.

AF FACTS

In 2004, Willie Apiata, nicknamed 'Mudguts', earned the Victoria Cross while serving with the New Zealand SAS in Afghanistan. He picked up his comrade and carried him 70 m across rocky ground, through enemy fire, to safety.

An airstrike on part of the Tora Bora mountains in Afghanistan.

After the airstrike, Special Forces patrols hid in the rocks to capture the survivors. On one occasion they were surprised by a large number of enemy fighters who were hiding in an underground bunker, but they managed to fight them off.

Special Forces work with local people, not only to find terrorists, but also to help get food and equipment.

"SAS troops carried illuminated bicycle flashers to mark themselves if shot, so they could easily be found in the smoke and confusion of battle." Ex-SAS soldier Andy McNab

Raiders from the sea

Special Forces units such as the US Navy SEALS attack from the sea. Patrols are carried to their target by submarines, fishing boats, landing craft or canoes.

Members of South Korea's navy commandos reach the seashore in their inflatable dinghy.

Special Boat Teams (SBTs) support SEAL units. This SBT is practising high-speed, shallow-water control.

These *Special Forces divers are practising how to attach mines underneath boats.*

Special Boat Teams are trained to find their way (navigate) at sea. They can use small boats, such as rigid raiders, zodiacs and dinghies, as well as mini-submarines. These teams are used for scouting and for seizing oil rigs and ships captured by pirates or terrorists.

Some teams parachute into the sea with their canoes, then paddle to shore. Diving teams swim underwater and use mini-submarines to pull them along. During direct action, they sneak into enemy harbours and attach magnetic mines to enemy ships.

"It can get hairy sometimes but I guess that's all part of the challenge, you have to be ready for it."
SB1 N. Palmer, US Navy

AF FACTS

Special Forces divers, or 'frogmen', use re-breather equipment. This allows them to breathe underwater but doesn't make bubbles on the surface like SCUBA gear.

Mission: Fighting gang crime

Special Operations teams are often used in the fight against pirates and criminal gangs.

In 2008, seven pirates captured a French yacht, *Carré d'As* (*Four Aces*), off the coast of Somalia, Africa. They demanded a €1 million ransom for the two hostages. Ten days later, the pirates woke to find themselves staring into the guns of a Special Forces team. It had flown over 7,000 km to rescue the hostages.

US Rangers use a Zodiac boat to practise the sort of swift raid needed to rescue hostages.

The frogmen dropped by parachute into the sea. Then they swam underwater towards the yacht, using re-breather equipment and night-vision goggles. They climbed aboard silently with ropes and lightweight grappling hooks, taking the pirates by surprise.

AF FACTS

In 2002, US Green Berets trained local military forces in the South American country of Colombia in the fight against powerful drug gangs. They trained them in night-fighting, scouting and using helicopters to drop patrols.

AF FACTS

In the early 1990s, Special Forces teams in Lithuania carried out a series of midnight raids on Mafia establishments, helping to put many major criminals behind bars.

Suspected Lithuanian Mafia members are arrested following raids by Special Forces.

Who Dares Wins

The challenges faced by the world's Special Forces are always changing. Lots of work goes into preparing for things that may happen in the future.

The Boeing A-160 Hummingbird is a new unmanned rotorcraft – also called a UAV.

It's likely that Special Forces will remain the eyes and ears of the armed services. Nothing beats having a patrol on the ground to watch the enemy and report back to base. However, in future unmanned aerial vehicles (UAVs) may carry out some of their attack missions.

AF FACTS

The Hummingbird can fly over 258 kph and make decisions on its own. Eventually it could be used to support units on the ground.

New equipment is being invented to help Special Forces teams in the future. This includes new boats and personal gear (see right).

The SAS motto sums up the spirit of the Special Forces, "Who Dares Wins".

Fast facts

The US Rangers were formed in 1754 under Major Robert Rogers. Travelling by foot and canoe across North America, they covered 650 km in 60 days without alerting their enemy, the Abernaki people.

One of the most secretive Special Forces units is the British Special Boat Service, which has around 120 regular operators and a small number of reserves. They were part of a team that rescued *New York Times* journalist Stephen Farrell after he was taken hostage by Taliban fighters in September 2009.

The SAS has taken part in more conflicts than any other Special Forces unit, including operations in Oman, Malaysia, Gambia, Falkland Islands, Colombia, Kuwait, Bosnia, Peru, Albania, Sierra Leone, Afghanistan and Iraq.

The South Korean counter-terrorist unit, the 707th Special Missions Battalion, has a team of female operatives used for undercover operations.

During the Cold War, Russian Special Forces units, known as Spetznaz, had a fearsome reputation. They were trained to assassinate senior NATO commanders and carry out attacks on missile bases and bridges.

Glossary

Airstrike – a military attack on a ground target from the air, usually made by a bomber or helicopter.

Ammunition – the bullets and shells fired from guns.

Artillery – heavy guns that fire shells over a long distance.

Avalanche – when large amounts of snow and ice slip down a mountain side.

Bushcraft – skills needed to survive in tough environments.

Camouflage – objects or colours used to help hide in an environment, such as a pattern on a uniform.

Communicate – to understand someone, and to be understood, usually through a shared language.

Conflict – an armed battle between two or more groups – on a smaller scale than a war.

Frostbite – frozen and blistered skin and tissue.

Infra-red – light invisible to the human eye. People use infra-red vision equipment to see in the dark.

Reconnaissance – searching and gathering information about the enemy, such as troop numbers.

Recruits – people who have just signed up to military training.

Resourceful – being clever and thinking clearly even in tough conditions, such as a war zone.

Sniper – a rifleman who hides himself to shoot at enemy soldiers, usually from a long distance.

Tactical – the use of skills involving moving and positioning to avoid or attack an enemy.

Terrain – a type of ground and conditions, such as rocky hills.

Victoria Cross – medal awarded to British troops for extreme bravery.

Websites

www.sealswcc.com

Home of the US Navy Seals that take their name
from the elements in which they operate – Sea, Air
and Land. Find out about their history, download
pictures and watch training videos.

www.whodareswins.com

A website with information about many of the
world's Special Forces units, including the SAS,
Delta Force and teams from Australia and New
Zealand. You can also watch clips of news reports
showing troops in action.

www.howstuffworks.com/green-beret.htm
and
www.howstuffworks.comdelta-force.htm

Everything you need to know about the Green
Berets, the US Army's Special Forces unit, and the
even more secretive Delta Force. Find out about
"The Ballad of the Green Berets" which became
a number 1 hit in the US in 1966.

www.french-foreign-legion.com

Learn about the history, traditions and code
of honour of this famous unit.

http://www.eliteukforces.info
A website dedicated to British Special Forces units. Read the latest headlines and watch videos of elite forces in action and training.

www.army.mod.uk/infantry/regiments/3471. aspx
The official website of the British Army Parachute Regiment, or Red Devils.

http://ausmilitary.com/SASRegiment.htm
The website of the Special Air Service Regiment, the most famous elite force in Australia.

http://www.goarmy.com/ranger
Find out what it takes to become a member of the US 75th Ranger Regiment.

http://juni0r.orconhosting.net.nz/nzsas.html
A site with lots of interesting information about the New Zealand Special Air Service, which has a reputation for producing some of the best combat trackers in the world.

Index